D0517174

Whitewater Kayaking

Edited by Dave Harrison

Illustrated by Bruce Morser

STACKPOLE BOOKS

0 11557 02723 5

Copyright © 1998 by Stackpole Books

Published by
STACKPOLE BOOKS
5067 Ritter Road
Mechanicsburg, PA 17055

All rights reserved, including the right to reproduce this book or portions thereof in any form or by any means, electronic or mechanical, including photocopying, recording, or by any information storage and retrieval system, without permission in writing from the publisher. All inquiries should be addressed to Stackpole Books, 5067 Ritter Road, Mechanicsburg, PA 17055.

Printed in the United States

First edition

10 9 8 7 6 5 4 3 2 1

Cover design by Tracy Patterson

Illustrations © 1990–1997 Bruce Morser. All rights reserved.

The material in this book originally appeared in *Canoe & Kayak* magazine. See page 60 for subscription information.

Library of Congress Cataloging-in-Publication Data

Whitewater kayaking / edited by David F. Harrison—1st ed.
    p.   cm.—(Canoe and kayak techniques)
    ISBN 0-8117-2723-8
    1. White-water canoeing. 2. Kayaking I. Harrison, David, 1938– . II. Series.
GV788.W55 1998
797.1'224—dc21   97-18079
                                        CIP

Contents

Contributors

Gordon Grant is the former head of instruction at the Nantahala Outdoor Center in Bryson City, North Carolina. He lives in Asheville, North Carolina.

Dave Harrison is the publisher of *Canoe & Kayak* magazine and author of *Canoeing* (Stackpole Books), and *Sea Kayaking Basics* (Hearst Marine Books).

Claudia Kerckhoff-van Wijk is a ten-time Canadian slalom champion and World Championship Bronze medalist. She is owner/director of the Madawaska Kanu Centre, a whitewater paddling school in Ontario, Canada.

Stephen U'Ren was a member of the United States Whitewater Team from 1984 to 1986. He is the author of *Performance Kayaking* (Stackpole Books) and lives in Seattle.

Bruce Morser, a Colgate University graduate who also holds a Master of Fine Arts from the University of Washington, has won many awards for his unique illustrating style. He lives on Vashon Island, Washington.

Introduction

Think of Meryl Streep crashing through rapids and a boiling kidnapping plot in *River Wild*. Think back further, to the teeth-clenching suspense of *Deliverance* and scenes designed to wake you up screaming in the middle of the night. Dramatic stuff, to be sure, but most whitewater enthusiasts are not just adrenaline-driven thrill seekers. They are explorers, visitors, really, who hope to experience the natural world in a hidden canyon or find harmony with the most dynamic of nature's forces: moving water.

The broadening appeal of this sport and the subsequent explosion in its popularity can be explained in this way: in whitewater, we've regained a sense of awe. Instead of a terrible force to contend with, an obstacle to progress, and the backdrop for the sinister, whitewater is now recognized as a way to discover the wonder of nature. Maneuvering through whitewater is an exhilarating experience in itself, but also a means to escape into canyons and gorges, along riverbanks, to places where the force and power of nature soon give way to tranquillity.

If you want to experience the beauty and thrill of whitewater, we want to provide the access: where to go, how to prepare, and, most important of all, how to have fun, safely. Yes, this sport involves risk, but your first job is to learn to assess risk, assess your own skills, and match the two. Whether you are the rankest beginner on a gentle river or an expert river runner, your goal is the same: to descend the river in control. We want to help you do that.

The Art of Control: Anticipation, Reaction, and Timing

by the editors of Canoe & Kayak *magazine*

No matter which vehicle you choose—canoe, kayak, or inflatable—for whitewater adventure, your objective is to get down the river *under control*. In paddling literature, you will find many articles describing specific techniques for directing and controlling both canoes and kayaks, but making a safe, controlled descent of a whitewater river involves a number of basic principles that are common to all river runners, regardless of their craft.

The first principle is to match the water to your skills. Whether you take formal instruction (which we strongly recommend) or attempt to teach yourself, basic novice skills must first be gained on flat—that is, non-moving—water. Such skills include entering and exiting your boat, the forward stroke, direction control, the wet exit (what to do when you tip over), and going in reverse. For direction control you must learn how to use the leverage of the paddle to "draw" and "pry" and especially how to make the boat go in a straight line. Since whitewater boats tend to be "directionally unstable," meaning that they have a mind of their own, that will be your first and greatest challenge.

Once you are able to make the boat go where you want it to—forward in a straight line, reverse, sideways, and through a buoy course—you need to learn blade control. Draw, pry, and sweep strokes must be learned on both sides of your canoe or kayak. Finally, you must learn to control your boat with boat leans and the use of bracing strokes, high and low. When and how you lean your boat is even more important than making the correct stroke.

I heard a cross-country skiing coach tell a class that they should learn techniques in slow motion: if they couldn't do it slow, they weren't going to be able to do it fast. Good advice for paddlers, too, which brings us to the second principle. Learn your strokes and moves on water a solid grade lower than the one you aspire to. In other words, learn class III moves on class II water. Jumping onto a more difficult river than you are ready for may test your survival skills but also may actually retard your learning progress.

In order to observe the first principle, you need to observe another: know the class and water level of the river you intend to run. Know what effects the water level has on the difficulty.

Be aware of hazards, like low dams, logs or downed trees, waterfalls, or other man-made obstructions. If any of these are present, you need to know how to get around them—lining, portaging—and where and when to get out of the boat to scout. Scouting is called for on any rapid rated Class II or greater, until your skill or experience can predict a safe passage, which brings us to another principle. Don't run any rapid that you don't think you could swim out of safely.

Now that you have advanced to the river appropriate to your skill level and are headed downstream, you will observe many other wise river-running principles. Assuming you have scouted your rapid, from either boat or shore, you need to "line up" your boat. Unless scouting dictates otherwise, generally try to stay with the main current and the deepest channel. This may mean following a "ramp" that leads into the biggest whitewater, and in fact avoiding those slick patches caused by water that's been interrupted.

There is no such thing as too many eddy turns. Eddies are where you truly control your descent. They can rescue you from chaos and give you a vantage point for scouting your next move.

Beginners must master the "ferry." The principle is simply this: the boat is moved sideways across the river current by angling the boat to that current, using enough power to offset the momentum of the current. That can be done with the nose of your boat either pointed downriver (a "back ferry") or pointed upstream (oddly, a "forward ferry"). Back and for-

ward refer to the paddle strokes, not the direction in which the boat is pointed. In fact, the most effective way to cross from one side of the river to the other is the forward ferry. You drive your boat, bow upstream, into the main current, paddling with just enough power and just the correct angle so that the current striking the bow of your boat pushes it sideways. The correct angle is determined by the force of the current; the more powerful the current, the less angle required to move you sideways.

Once you have scouted your route, lined up the boat, and entered the rapid, entering and leaving eddies and ferrying are the primary means of controlling your descent.

Here are a few other principles that river runners observe. Your worst enemies on a river are wood and man-made obstructions. Rocks are pretty harmless; if you are going to hit one, lean *into* it. In fact, when in peril, lean the boat downstream; that is, you want to present the bottom of your boat to oncoming currents. Learn to recognize "holes" and eddy lines. In the case of the former, avoidance is best, but be especially wary of those whose "smile" faces upstream. If the smile is a downstream "frown," you can usually escape out the ends. The strength of the eddy lines is determined by the river's steepness and water levels, and the more powerful the eddy line, the wider the angle at which it must be attacked.

The Forgotten Forward Stroke

Dave Harrison

The problem with whitewater is that moving water may give the paddler the illusion of a competent forward stroke. If you're in line with the current headed downstream, a little flick of the wrist, a slight push/pull of the elbows, and *hey!* I'm a river rocket!

Believe me. It is an illusion. A powerful, efficient, and properly executed forward stroke is usually the difference between a good kayaker and a great one. Here are a few good reasons why: First, a solidly planted forward stroke is the best brace you've got. Second, your body and paddle are well forward, and that's where the power is. It's also the place to be for executing most of the other important strokes. Third, it's the stroke which gets you into position for entering an eddy, the stroke with which you leave an eddy, the secret to getting on a surfing wave and just about anywhere you need to be. Finally, the torso rotation that goes into a good forward stroke is a critical component of virtually all of your other kayak strokes.

Here's what to do: Extend your paddle in front of you over the deck. Keep your left elbow straight as you pull back the right hand, like a pitcher's windup. Your torso should wind up to the right, too. The object of the game is to plant the left blade as far forward in the water as possible, and to do so with torso rotation and arm extension—not by bending forward. Now, plant the blade and pull the boat to the blade as you "unwind" your torso, and punch out your upper arm. The punching out of your upper arm should also be part of the paddle stroke; use your extended left hand as a fulcrum for applying force to your "lever" (the paddle shaft). Your left arm stays straight throughout the stroke, until you bend it to pick up the blade for the right-side stroke. End your stroke as the paddle blade reaches your hips, and if you really rotated your torso—rather than merely articulating your elbows—your blade comes out of the water still perpendicular to the water and pointed away from the boat.

Here are two good tricks for getting powerful strokes that use your strong back and shoulder muscles, not wimpy arm muscles: first, watch your PFD's zipper. It should move from side to side, which indicates that you are moving your torso. Second, look at your elbow after punching out your arm for the new blade plant. It should be straight. Simply moving the elbows back and forth is no substitute for torso rotation. It works, but it results in a weak stroke and sore elbows.

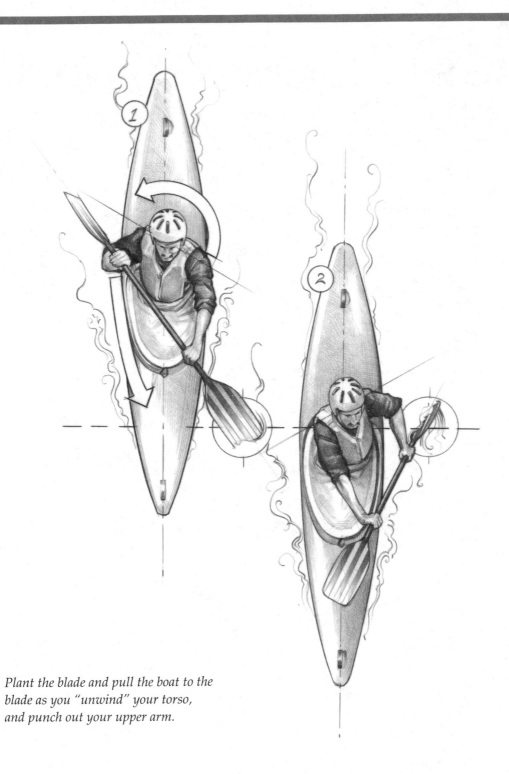

Plant the blade and pull the boat to the
blade as you "unwind" your torso,
and punch out your upper arm.

The Sweep Stroke: A New Look

Gordon Grant

What differentiates the expert paddlers from the rest of us mere mortals is their ability to precisely and perfectly execute the most basic of strokes in all situations. The flaw in this pronouncement is that there is often disagreement among the experts on exactly how these basic strokes should be done.

Recently, I had an eye-opening revelation on the execution of one of the most elementary strokes in the kayaker's repertoire, the forward sweep. Now, I like to think that I am open to any and all new ideas that periodically move through the sport, but I was convinced that one stroke I really knew how to do was the forward sweep.

Rotate your body forward, plant the paddle by your feet with arms kept low, and sweep the paddle out and back in the widest possible arc. Then, if the boat fails to turn, you simply rely on the stern draw (the back half of the forward sweep) to "catch" the boat's circular momentum and return you to the straight and narrow.

Right?

Wrong, said none other than multiple world kayak champions Richard Fox and Miriam Jerusalmi. They were the headliners at a youth coaching conference which I was attending. The purpose of the sweep, they said, is to provide turning power without slowing the boat; any movement of the paddle with its emphasis behind the boater would have a retarding effect on the boat's speed. Racers do not like to have their speed reduced for any reason.

Here's the sweep stroke technique recommended by Fox and Jerusalmi:

If you are making a forward sweep on the right side, for example, you should make a definite, conscious effort *not* to move the paddle back, but rather, straight out and away from the boat. This will cause the non-sweeping hand—in this case, the left—to punch across the center line of the boat. Place the paddle at the beginning of the stroke as you normally would, and emphasize an outward rather than a backward movement of the blade. This will definitely feel odd at first, to change a lifetime of habit, but you will be amazed at how quickly the boat comes around. This stroke is especially effective in a situation for which I have invariably prescribed the stern draw—that is, correcting a too-great ferry angle. Try this sweep as you enter the current from an eddy at too-open an angle. Done properly, the stroke will correct your angle *and* increase your speed across the current.

The Duffek Without Defects

Gordon Grant

At some point in their careers, paddlers are confronted with the stroke with a name of its own: the Duffek. Many boaters, even the quick learners, find this stroke very awkward to learn. They tie their arms in knots, tip over and sputter to the surface pronouncing the stroke weird, or useless.

It doesn't have to be. The Duffek, or hanging draw, is a wonderfully efficient stroke. With it, paddlers can pivot their boats in a single stroke with minimum loss of speed. While most often used by boaters to snap a crisp eddy turn or peel out, it can also be used for adjustments of angle while going at high speed through a

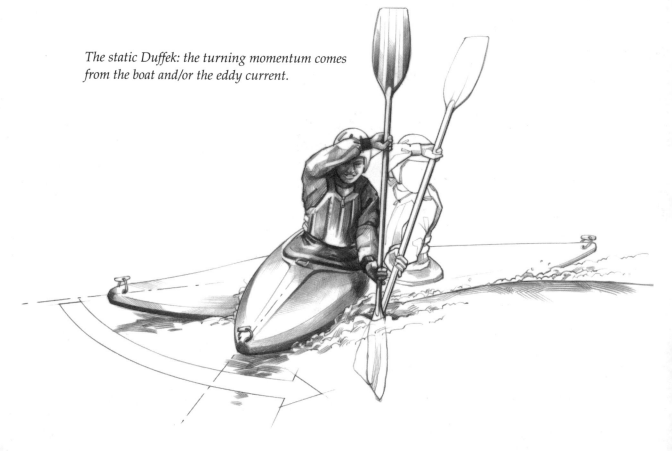

The static Duffek: the turning momentum comes from the boat and/or the eddy current.

rapid. If you remember these basics, you'll have no trouble learning the stroke, or refining the one you already have.

The first step in learning this stroke is performed without a paddle. For a Duffek to the right, do the following: Make an L with your right arm, the elbow lightly touching your side. Bring your left hand up and across your chest, and rest it on your right shoulder. Now, and only now, rotate your whole body as far to the right as is comfortable. Repeat this motion until it feels natural and smooth. This is the basic motion of the stroke. You can adjust the "feel" of it by moving your right or left hand slightly away from your body. You can play considerably with the height and angle of the top (in this case, left) hand, moving it out until it is almost directly over the lower hand. The lower arm should stay well bent and fairly close to the side. Practice this motion to the opposite side. Do it until it feels relaxed.

Now you should pick up your paddle. Replicate the motions you have learned, and think of setting the paddle in the water, rather than moving it. You should feel the resistance in your stomach and back rather than your elbow joints. The problem most people have with the Duffek is extending their lower arm out too much, which makes the stroke awkward.

Feel free to move your hands around to find the position most comfortable for you. It doesn't really matter whether you find yourself looking over or under your top arm, whatever works best for you. The last touch of the stroke lies in the wrist on the side of the blade in the water. Roll your wrist back for more bite and turn, or roll it forward for less drag on the water. The important thing is once the paddle is set, *do not* move it toward the boat! Tense your stomach muscles, and let the boat turn toward the paddle.

Setting the paddle is essential. You either have to be going faster than the water, or set the paddle in the water that is flowing against it. With this concept in mind, you'll tighten up your eddy turns, and look more like a stylish descendant of the gifted Hungarian slalom racer who introduced it in the fifties. GO!

The Reverse Sweep

Claudia Kerckhoff-van Wijk

Before the invention of the Duffek stroke, the reverse sweep was the preferred method for turning a kayak. Technique discussions often overlook it, but this stroke is highly effective when done properly. The most practical application for the reverse sweep is when turning the boat quickly in the middle of the current; it is seldom used to enter and exit eddies because it slows the boat down too much.

Start your reverse sweep by rotating your torso 45 degrees to the turning side.

Place your paddle parallel to your kayak and keep your leading arm (the arm near the stern) totally straight. Always keep your leading arm straight throughout the sweep, which forces the blade to follow a wide path. If properly executed, one sweep should turn the boat a full 180 degrees. Look at the blade closest to the stern and make sure the non-power face is facing out. Always use the non-power face of the blade. Place your weight onto the shaft and push the blade out perpendicu-

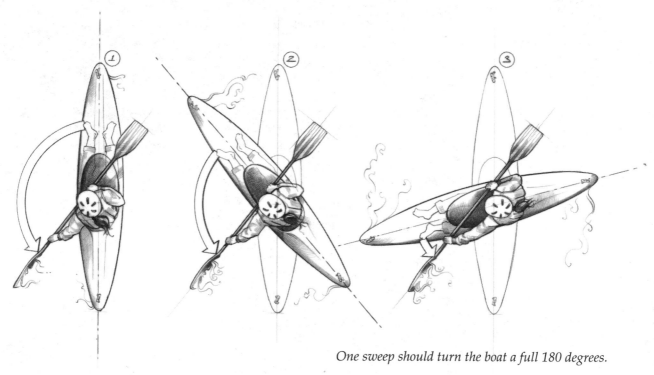

One sweep should turn the boat a full 180 degrees.

lar to your stern. Be sure to lean your body, not the boat, onto the stroke by disjointing at the waist. Good upper-body flexibility is important to perform this, and many other, kayaking maneuvers. Force the blade's path around in a giant semicircle all the way toward the bow, using the strength of your torso, not just your arms, to power the turn. Keep your paddle blade fully submerged, but always visible just below the water surface.

Your boat must remain flat (not on the edge) throughout this turn to maximize the efficiency of your turn in the middle of the current. Whitewater boats are designed to spin best when kept flat at the point where the least amount of boat is touching the water. The exception to this rule is when using the reverse sweep to make a tight turn out of an eddy while staying on the eddy line. Here, you want to use your body to tilt the boat downstream to keep the current from catching the upstream edge of the boat.

An extension of the turn initiated with a reverse sweep is to combine it with the forward sweep. This combination provides the fastest way to turn the boat. I also use this stroke combination to spin the boat in on-water warm-ups, especially when sitting in a small eddy above a nerve-racking rapid.

The key to an effective reverse sweep is to lean your body onto your strokes and concentrate on blade placement into the water as close to the ends of the boat as possible. The further you reach away from the center of the turn, the more turning power you have. The result: greater boat control.

The reverse sweep is both a stable and a powerful move when performed correctly and one that you will grow to enjoy out on the river.

Back Ferries: Stepping Stones to Being Honed

Gordon Grant

The back ferry is an often neglected skill in the kayaker's repertoire. Perfecting your back ferry will enhance your sense of balance, refine your boat leans, and lead to more advanced skills, such as back surfing on waves. Learning the move is a two-part process, with the final test being the ability to exit an eddy (stern first) and move across the river.

PART ONE: A DUFFEK THAT MOVES

Try it first on easy flat water—flat, but fairly swift. Be sure to begin in the center of the river, facing downstream. Start back-paddling to slow yourself down. Let your boat gradually swing sideways so that the stern is pointing toward the river, right shore. Follow these steps:

1. Rotate your body into position for a good Duffek, fully rotated toward the right, with both hands out over the water. Here is the difference: In a Duffek, the lower arm stays bent and close to the body. In the corrective draw for the back ferry, you will reach your lower arm almost to full extension. Be sure to keep a light bend at the elbow.

2. Put the blade in the water at an angle of 45 degrees from the boat. If the bow of your boat is twelve o'clock, your lower arm is pointed between one and two (or ten and eleven on the left).

3. Put the blade fully in the water and unwind from your rotation, pulling powerfully toward your feet.

4. To finish the stroke, rotate your lower hand forward (straightening the wrist), and either lift the paddle out to the side, or keep it in the water and feather it out for another draw stroke.

The effect of this stroke should be identical to that of a well-placed stern draw on a regular front ferry; you should feel the boat swing around so that it is again parallel with the current. At this point, resume backward paddling. As the boat begins to swing sideways again, repeat the bow draw to "catch" the angle before it becomes too great. Work both directions from the center of the river and on easy water. Mastery will only come from practice, including graduation to whitewater of increasing power before you attempt to back ferry out of an eddy.

PART TWO: LEAVING THE EDDY

1. Be sure to line up parallel to the eddy line. Starting too deep in the eddy will invariably result in too much angle and a blown ferry.

2. Look over one shoulder only, the current side. With several strong back-strokes, paddle up the eddy.

3. The moment your stern crosses the eddy line, rotate strongly into your bow draw on the current (downstream) side and pull toward your feet. Timed properly, this will "catch" the boat as your body crosses the eddy line and prevent you from being swung sideways. You should be well out in the current with a minimal angle. Continue to backpaddle to maintain your position, throwing in a few draws if the boat angle widens, and glide to the far shore with a studied lack of concern.

You've taken a new step toward whitewater kayaking mastery, balanced and in control, and are ready to attempt other, even more challenging moves.

Use the cross-bow draw to achieve the correct ferry angle.

The "Hairy" Ferry

Stephen U'Ren

Picture yourself deep in a steep gorge, in an eddy against a sheer wall, above a log-choked nightmare of a drop. As you squint through the logs you see some rising mist. Better get to the portage route on the other side of the river. At this water level it's an easy ferry, as long as you don't panic.

The next weekend you're paddling the same river, only the water is a *lot* higher. Approaching the log jam you've spaced out and gotten yourself in the same eddy as before, and you have to do the same ferry only under more complicated and difficult circumstances.

(Although you're forced to ferry, first look downstream and try to find the most viable Plan B *if* you were to blow the ferry. *Don't* sit there and meditate on worst-case scenarios; *do* give yourself every option possible.)

Before you start, examine the current. Beware of surging waves and boils, and consider the waves' shapes and angles (relative to the current). For your ferry, look for a wave to surf across, preferably one as far upstream in the wave chain as you think you can make. Not only is this usually the biggest wave, but you could catch the next wave in line if you fall off the top one. If clearly the most "surfable" wave is lower on the wave chain, take that one.

Now swallow that bile and focus your mind. Start low in the eddy and paddle hard, but don't flail wildly across the current. The key is to catch a wave and stay on it—even if it's small—and let it help you across.

If the wave is not angled to the current and "non-surgy," the ferry shouldn't be too hard. If the wave angles in mid current, it'll be trickier. If the wave angles upstream, you'll have to *really* paddle hard (you may need to take strokes only on your downstream side). If it angles downstream, you'll need to slow down a little and drift backward slightly while continuing to surf the wave. This is a tenuous balance: Too much power with your forward strokes and you'll pearl and ender out; too little and you'll drift off the wave entirely.

If the current or wave is surging, be very aggressive and make certain you don't wobble or lose your ferry angle. If you're on a wave and it surges and steepens, quickly lean back to raise your bow, use a backstroke/rudder, lean your boat toward your destination, and flatten your ferry angle (all these maneuvers prevent pearling). Conversely, if your wave betrays you and vanishes from beneath you, paddle like crazy: Either get to shore or try to stay in place long enough for the wave to reappear under you.

Nearing the end of your ferry, spin slightly perpendicular to the current, as

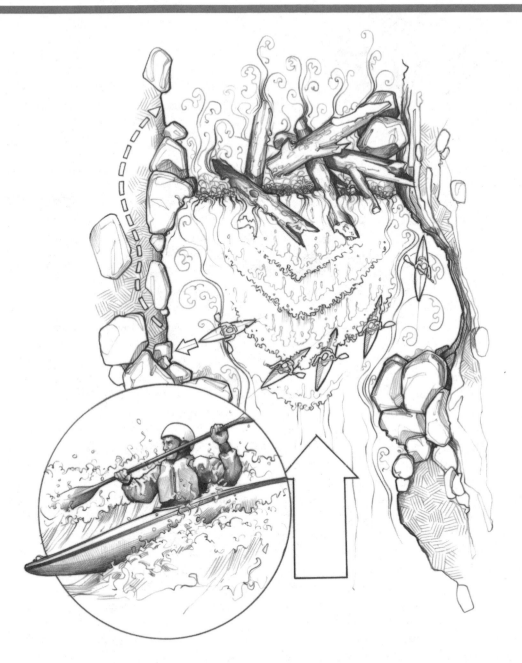

you will need a good angle to enter the eddy well. There are few worse things than ferrying across with style only to spin out and get stalled on a boiling eddy line.

Remember: If you practice "hairy" ferries above benign spots, you'll be a heck of a lot more comfortable at them when you have to do them for real.

Back-Surfing

Stephen U'Ren

Imagine surfing a wave with your eyes closed. In lieu of vision you have to rely on your kinesthetic senses of balance and momentum and react quickly and appropriately.

This, in essence, is what back-surfing is about. When you're facing downstream, you can see only where you are on the wave—a valuable clue—but not how the wave is breaking and moving behind you. In spite of this apparent handicap, back-surfing can be surprisingly easy and fun, at least after you get the feel for it. Your other senses will compensate for the paucity of visual input.

Getting established on the wave is the toughest part. Start at an easy, non-surging wave abutting an eddy. You could attempt to drift downstream onto a wave while paddling backwards, but this is not the best way to begin, as the current is invariably stronger than you think. It's *much* easier to begin by paddling backwards up an eddy with much the same angle and speed (and lean) you would use to initiate a front-surf.

When you're first learning to back-surf, it's easy to get too much angle and get surfed clean off the other side of the wave. To avoid this, minimize your angle to the eddy line and back-paddle up the eddy in a nearly straight line. This may be tougher than you think; most boaters don't paddle backwards much and con-stantly need to correct and re-correct direction, at least at first.

To get onto the wave and stay there, boat lean is critical. As with front-surfing, you want your boat to be leaned downstream most of the time. Keep your body position slightly forward (more so on steeper waves) to prevent your stern from pearling and to aid your tracking ability.

As soon as you get on the wave, place either a reverse sweep on your non-entry (toward the opposite bank from which you entered) side or a quick front rudder on your entry side to push you up onto the wave and then stabilize your position (you may need to do both in rapid succession). Remember that all your steering strokes are done way up at the bow, the downstream end. Execute the front-rudder stroke by placing the paddle near your feet, at the same position you use to initiate a forward sweep. Keep your paddle low and forward, forward arm extended, and blade power face out with the back edge right next to the boat.

Use the front rudder to cut back and forth on the wave. (The more cutting you do on the wave face, the less likely it is you will pearl.) Pulling this stroke toward you will cause the boat to turn to the side of the stroke. However, it's often easier to initiate a front-rudder turn with a subtle and brief upstream lean (or off-side lean, if you prefer) which you quickly and

To approach the wave, back-paddle up the eddy in a nearly straight line. Once you're on the wave, use a front-rudder stroke (inset) to maneuver.

smoothly convert to a downstream lean. If you start to drift off the wave's backside, lean back and back-paddle like mad, and work to push your butt back down into the trough. You'll get your center of gravity off the crest of the wave.

After you've learned to get on the wave by backing up onto it, another, slicker way to get on the wave is to paddle forward up the eddy, ease onto the eddy line, let the current spin you 180 degrees, and use a powerful reverse sweep to push yourself onto the wave. The back-surf can be incredibly frustrating at first, but you'll be amazed at how fast you catch on.

Fine-Tune Your Sweep Roll

Gordon Grant

All good rolls share similarities of technique: They tend to be executed with the emphasis on the movement of the body rather than the paddle, and therefore bring the paddler to the surface with the minimum of effort. Let's correct one of the recurrent problems of students of the sweep-type roll, punching up or out with the back hand. Which is the back hand? Set up for a roll where your right hand will be the control hand throughout. In your set-up, twist to the right, lean forward, and put both hands, knuckles down, in the water beside the boat. As you

Rev your motorcycle to tune up your sweep roll.

can see, your left hand is your leading hand, and your right, your back hand.

"Back hand punch out" is a common error that results when the paddler straightens the back arm either up or forward when the kayak is most of the way up from the roll. It feels like you're getting more power this way, but no. It causes the angle of the paddle to change, either to sink or to quickly tuck to the stern. In both cases, the paddle goes down quickly and the roll is lost, frustrating the paddler who had felt so close to success.

Once upside down, concentrate only on these things: Before you leave your set-up position, move your leading hand about a foot away from the boat. Not up or down—away. Think of separating the hand from the boat. Once this is done, the movements are simple and done together. Think of "revving up a motorcycle" with your right hand. Roll the knuckles back and bring the hand up as tight as you can to your right shoulder, and sit up as you do so. Your leading hand continues its movement away from the boat, and even with eyes closed, your head follows the track of the leading hand. You will find yourself sitting upright with amazing ease. When your eyes open, you will be looking at your left hand. The paddle will be about level with your shoulders, and your right arm will be a tight V, with the knuckles close to the shoulder. Easy, wasn't it? You just reduced the motions to the essential.

Up Your Boat Without a Paddle

Claudia Kerckhoff-van Wijk

If your paddling adventures ever take you up the proverbial creek—the one without the paddle—you'll be happy you took some time to master the hands-only roll. Not only is it an impressive maneuver, it is a practical move in a tight situation, when you do lose your paddle in a river.

The late fall and winter seasons offer the ideal time to learn the hands-only roll. When it starts getting too cold to paddle outside, and ice starts forming on the river banks, you can stay limber in your kayak by moving indoors to a swimming pool. A pool is really the best place to learn this move, since the warm clear water alleviates much of the anxiety of being upside down in your boat.

There are many ways to perform a hands-only roll, but the one I find most reliable in action is the sculling version. I have broken this technique into its two basic elements: the hip flick and the sculling motion. The successful hands-only roll involves the concurrent blending of these two moves.

THE HIP FLICK

Begin by practicing your hip flick, either off the side of the pool or with a partner. First, tip your boat over and submerse your head completely (look at the bottom of the pool and keep your eyes open to stay oriented). From the upside-down position, flip the boat up, using only your hips and knees and keeping hand pressure to a minimum. Force up with the lower knee and down with the other. Keep your head low and keep your eyes focused on the bottom of the pool. When righting the boat, make sure that the boat comes up first, then your body, and lastly your head. Concentrate on keeping your shoulders square with the boat and using very little pressure on your hands. Your knees and hips should do most of the work.

SCULLING

The second step in mastering the hands-only roll involves integrating a sculling motion with your hands with the flip move described above. Cup your hands and practice sculling back and forth. Think of yourself as a synchronized swimmer, sculling with both hands in unison. This motion is exactly like treading water, but you hold your arms above your head rather than at the sides of your body.

THE ROLL

On your own, flip completely over again. Let your body float as close to the surface as possible, keeping your shoulders on the same level with the boat, which means you really have to twist at the waist. Cup your hands above your head and slowly scull in a continuous, controlled rhythm.

Flick your hips and continue to scull with your hands in unison. Keep sculling while the boat flips upright. The successful performance of a hands-only roll is dependent on maintaining your sculling rhythm and keeping your head down; it should be the last part out of the water. Don't stop sculling until your boat is completely upright.

Success rests on not panicking and losing the sculling rhythm nor forcing your head out of the water early. Take advantage of the winter to go indoors and practice this move and to get comfortable hanging upside down underwater. By the start of next paddling season you'll be a hot dog on the river and you'll also be prepared should you ever find yourself up the creek.

It's all in the hips and knees.

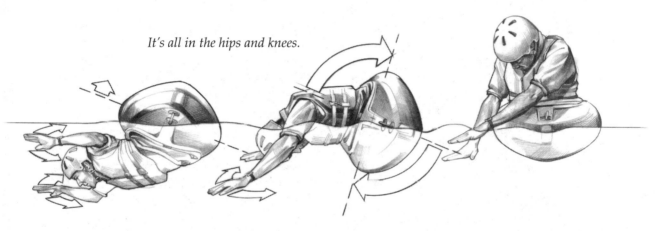

C-1 Insights for the Kayaker

Claudia Kerckhoff-van Wijk

When I was in training for whitewater slalom competitions, I learned a great deal by observing and imitating other paddlers. I always tried to train with more advanced paddlers because they were positive role models and I believed that a paddler can become as good as the people he or she paddles with.

However, I often found it difficult to imitate male kayakers whose maneuvers were often products of sheer strength—something my skinny arms and 125-pound frame didn't contain in quite the same measure. Frustrated by this, my attention shifted to learning from my immediate paddling buddies, the USA's hot C-1ers: John Lugbill, Bob Robinson, Kent Ford, and Davey Hearn. These paddlers were extremely fit and strong, but compared to kayakers, they had the disadvantage of paddling only one side of the boat and with a single blade. They needed to use the water more to their advantage and they had to be more precise when placing their boats. These were areas I needed to concentrate on as well, to make up for my strength handicap.

With practice, I learned their C-1 tricks and my paddling improved immensely. I share two techniques that had the greatest impact on my paddling: body movement and underwater turning strokes.

By body movement I am referring to the action of throwing your torso weight into a stroke maneuver. A good place to employ active body movement is in a common river situation: leaving an eddy to begin a forward ferry, especially if you are faced with a strong eddy fence (the wall of water in the main current substantially higher than the water level of the eddy itself).

To initiate a precise and efficient ferry, your boat speed and angle as you exit the eddy are important, but here is an additional trick: As soon as the kayak's nose is about to hit the current, stroke (on the current side) with your body leaning forward with the stoke. Complete this stroke with full power and abruptly force your torso to the back of the boat. This action lifts the bow of your boat out of the water and lets it glide across the surface of the current. Put in a few strong forward strokes on both sides of the kayak and lean your torso forward, in an aggressive position. This will confirm your control of the boat in the main current.

The initial stroke is the most important, and the more abrupt the change in the body position, the higher the bow will jump. If there is a smooth wave to surf across, which is often the case, then the first stroke may be the only one you need. I call this efficient paddling!

Another river situation where body movement is useful is in surfing a wave. Muscle paddlers who can power their way onto a wave may have an edge, but power paddling defeats the beauty of surfing, which is in the relaxing motion and the

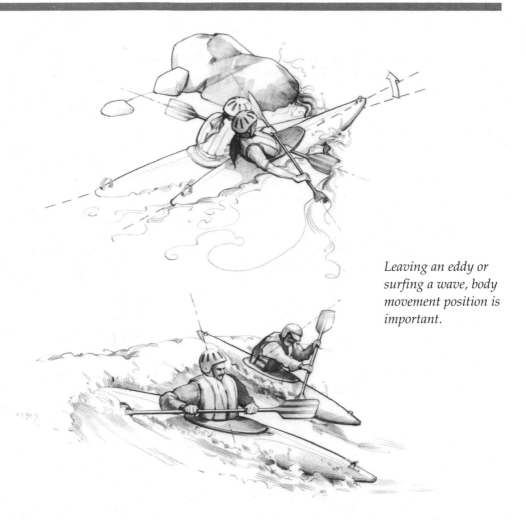

Leaving an eddy or surfing a wave, body movement position is important.

excitement of using the water's force to your full advantage.

It takes practice to find the "sweet spot"—the prime surfing point in the wave—but a back-and-forth body motion will help. To get the most out of a wave, lean your body forward as you paddle and slide into the wave trough to start surfing. This will keep the boat in the trough instead of getting swept downstream with the current. When the bow looks as though it is about to submerge, lean back so that your head is almost touching the back deck. Maintain a forward stroke and, if necessary, lean and put in a few forward paddling strokes to regain your position. Try leaning back again. You will have to lean back on very steep waves, but the more moderate waves offer the opportunity to move back and forth. It's also fun to move the boat up and down the wave trough without any paddling strokes, by using only your body movement. Soon, you'll be showing off as you twirl your paddle in the air to prove that you have mastered this technique.

More C-1 Insights for Kayakers

Claudia Kerckhoff-van Wijk

In another article I described the body action and boat positioning employed by C-1 paddlers to compensate for their one-side, one-blade disadvantage. Now, we'll see how a kayaker can apply the principle of a C-1 paddler's underwater turning stroke to his/her advantage in whitewater.

In observing C-1 paddlers, I have noticed that they can paddle quite a distance without lifting their paddles from the water. This does not mean that they are drifting uncontrollably. Rather, they are making small and crucial underwater strokes. In fact, the more contact the paddle has with the water, the greater the control of the boat.

To learn these underwater turning strokes in a kayak, first set up a flatwater practice site with a fixed object or buoy. This could be a slalom gate (simply a furring strip hung from a wire), or a floating object, like a plastic bottle tied to a rock, to maneuver around. Your objective will be to maneuver or rotate your boat tightly around the object without touching it and without removing your paddle from the water.

Try this first with your stronger paddling side and in a forward direction so you can see where you are going. Place the paddle in the water at about two o'clock (10 o'clock if you start on your left side), with the blade (power face) open toward the bow. Draw the paddle toward the bow in a Duffek-like stroke and pull the boat around in a circle. Next, slice the paddle back through the water to where you started the stroke, and repeat the exercise several times until the boat starts turning on the spot. Be sure to keep the blade in the water. A few small forward strokes will be needed to successfully maneuver the boat around the pole or buoy. Recover your stroke by slicing the blade back through the water; then, continue to draw your strokes into the bow to execute a tight turn around the object.

You can consider yourself successful with this stroke once you have completed three clean rotations around the object without hitting it. But don't get too cocky yet; try rotating around the same object using the opposite blade and see how you do. Another challenge is to try it backward by dragging your paddle to the kayak's stern in a reverse Duffek stroke.

This sculling stroke technique will help improve your paddling precision. It is also a great warm-up exercise to work on in the pool at the start of a rapid. Practice weaving around imaginary objects by using just one side of the paddle; avoid the temptation to use the opposite blade. It isn't that easy, and your respect for C-1 paddlers will definitely increase after you give it a few tries.

Apart from being a challenging exercise, this underwater turning stroke can be quite useful for kayakers in whitewater. Once you have mastered it, you will find that there are often situations in the middle of a rapid that warrant minute, but quick, turning strokes to avoid an oncoming rock or hydraulic. If you find yourself in this situation, execute a few underwater turning strokes. Remember to leave the paddle in the water and to position the boat so that you can paddle right around the object without hitting it. On your eddy turns, such a maneuver is sometimes referred to as a Duffek-to-forward stroke, and is the ultimate control move.

Consider yourself successful when you have completed three clean rotations—in each direction.

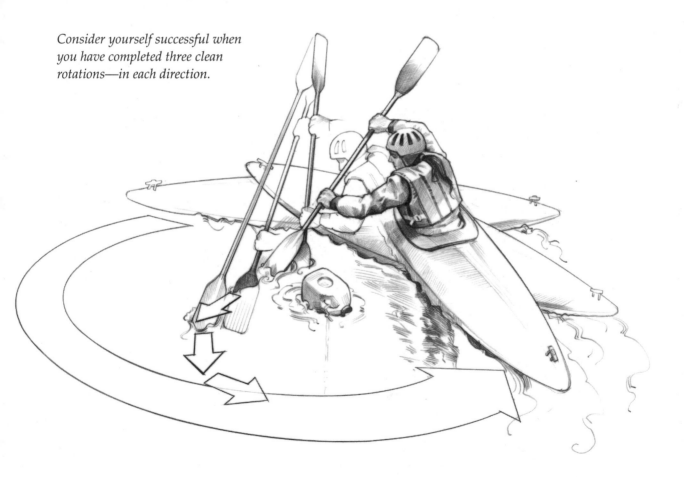

Rapid Resolution

Gordon Grant

Two of the activities I love best are rock climbing and river running, activities that have similar appeal, with the most obvious being the presence of some form of risk. Even on a moderate climb or on a class II river you are exposed to hazards and some measure of risk. Many of us derive our pleasure from recognizing and accepting the risks inherent in these sports; then, we take the challenge by exercising good technique and good judgment.

I read in a paddler's newsletter of the North Texas River Runners an excellent comment that went something like this: "Good judgment comes from experience, and you gain experience from making bad judgments." This is quite true, but in the sport today we are witnessing a growing number of paddlers whose technical paddling skills build up faster than their judgment.

Here is a mental process which, in my experience, whitewater paddlers will find to be pretty bomb-proof when it comes to making decisions about running a rapid. The technique is as important as your paddle strokes or your roll: It is the application of a series of critical questions you should ask yourself before running any rapid about which you have doubts. Really, these mental checks should take place before any rapid. The fact is, many avoidable accidents have taken place in rapids that were not considered terribly

difficult by those running them. The checklist usually takes seconds. On serious rapids it may take much longer. But it is always a necessary part of deciding whether to "go for it" or not.

Here's the checklist:

1. WHAT MOVES ARE REQUIRED TO RUN THIS RAPID?

Does it require a tough ferry on a breaking wave to thread two holes, or a diagonal "boof" move off a high drop? Maybe there is a wave that might knock me over; can I roll there?

2. CAN I DO THOSE MOVES?

This means, can I consistently do that move to the point where I am guaranteed of making it in this case?

3. WHAT ARE THE CONSEQUENCES IF I MISS THE REQUIRED MOVES?

Does the water push me toward any hazards: logs, undercuts, or a long swim through continuous rapids?

4. AM I WILLING TO ACCEPT THOSE CONSEQUENCES?

This is the biggest one of all. Having looked at all the risks, you must ask yourself if you are willing to deal with the consequences. This is true whether the rapid is a class III or a VI. If you are not willing to accept the consequences, it's time to

If you are not willing to accept the consequences, it's time to carry the rapid.

carry the rapid, and that will always be the right judgment for that rapid on that day.

Hey, some people might say, isn't this a little heavy? No, just honest, for it gives you a clarity of focus on what you can do. This doesn't mean I never run rapids where I am uncertain of the results; it just means that I have paid attention to the consequences. I used to paddle at a spot called Gregg Shoals, where we would fling ourselves into the biggest holes I have ever surfed. However, I knew that a swim would be just that; the rapids emptied into a long stretch of flatwater.

If each paddler answered this checklist with complete honesty, we would have fewer people running rapids just because they saw a buddy do it: "Well, Marvin did fine, and he was upside down through the last half!" Unlike a climbing ascent, a suc-cessful paddle descent of a rapid at your limits can be largely due to luck. Gravity and momentum serve both the intermediate and the expert alike. We have all seen paddlers of marginal skill sail through a drop cleanly, when moments before or immediately following, we watched an expert get completely thrashed. This rarely happens in climbing; it is hard to stumble and fall upwards.

If you follow the mental checklist above, you are using your own judgment, not just blindly following another person's lead—even if that person is a highly qualified instructor. No matter how good your companions are, they cannot paddle your boat for you. Personal judgment and decisions are much of what the joy of the sport is all about. Exercise this power and harness the joy for yourself.

The Angle on Eddy Turns

Stephen U'Ren

For cruising around on whitewater, probably the single most important skill is the ability to hit an eddy. Eddies are little havens for downstream scouting, spots to rest, plus they are awesome to rocket into.

Getting an optimal angle to the eddy line is the key to a good eddy turn, and traditionally, 45 to 90 degrees has been the angle to shoot for. A 45-degree angle will get you into the eddy. But it won't allow you to nail the turn the way a 90 will.

By far the best way to get this 90-degree angle is to set up in advance by taking a wide approach to the eddy, even though it takes you on a longer path than it would if you came straight toward it from upstream. Going wide also allows you to generate sufficient boat momentum for punching through the eddy line. Too often, boaters try to come straight down on the eddy and turn at the last moment. They need a last-second mega-sweep on the downstream side to get into the eddy. It's difficult and inefficient to use such a sweep, as it stalls the boat, preventing the boat from shooting deep into the eddy where the eddy turn is best done.

When you hit an eddy at 90 degrees, chances are you will not need any sort of sweep on the downstream side to punch through. A sweep at this angle could be detrimental, causing the boat to eddy-out too soon. A forward stroke in lieu of a downstream sweep should be sufficient. Then, once you cross the eddy line, place your turning Duffek to complete the eddy turn, but don't pull on the stroke until you're deep in the eddy where the boat turns best.

You can modify your approach for micro- and mega-sized eddies. You can essentially ferry into an eddy too small to allow a boat to turn into it by going extremely wide for the set-up. Turn your Duffek into a forward stroke to ensure that you don't slide out the bottom of the eddy. A second approach is to hit the eddy line at 60 to 90 degrees and use a short, powerful reverse stroke on your upstream side to spin the boat upstream and prevent it from flying through the eddy or pitoning the bank. You can feather the reverse stroke on the upstream side (without taking the blade out of the water) into a forward stroke, again, to keep from floating out of the eddy.

Hitting, and getting deep into, a monster eddy can be difficult, especially if it has a boily eddy line (it probably will). The trick is to cross the eddy line at 90 degrees and with lots of momentum. Because of the enormous strength of this type of eddy, it will tend to make you eddy-out on the eddy line, sending you spinning. (Get ready to brace!)

To keep this from happening, do a powerful sweep stroke on the upstream side as you cross the eddy line instead of

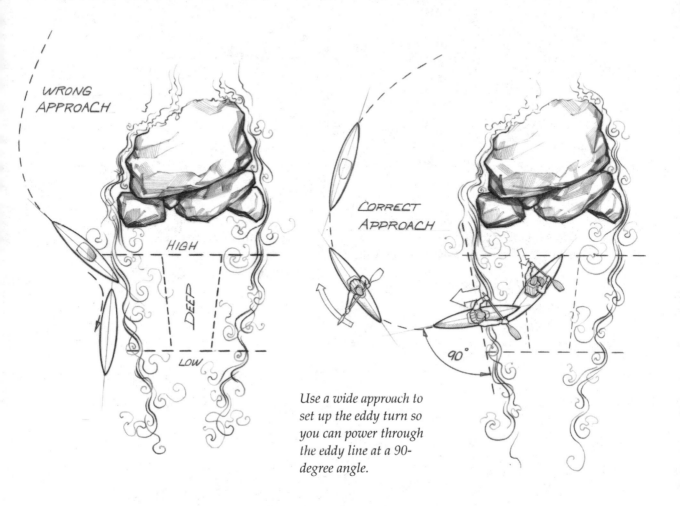

Use a wide approach to set up the eddy turn so you can power through the eddy line at a 90-degree angle.

doing a Duffek. You may sometimes need two or three consecutive sweeps if your angle is too far upstream or the eddy is strong. You can always do your turning Duffek when you are in the deeper, calmer area of the eddy.

While boat angle is the key to hitting eddies, remember your boat lean and experiment with boat speed. Experiment with how much speed is optimal for a given boat angle—in a particular eddy. Also play around with placing your Duffek at different spots in the eddy. In general, you will want to do it when you are deeper in the eddy than you may initially think is best. See for yourself.

Catching Recirculating Eddies

Stephen U'Ren

Executing a turn in an eddy that has a strong upstream flow requires some special considerations. Let's analyze such an eddy to gain strategic insight.

The most common place to see an eddy is behind a rock that's right next to shore. You can also find them on the upstream side of a solid outcropping. In this case, fast current rushes headlong into the outcropping, gets deflected toward shore, then travels upstream along the bank, and finally heads downstream as it blends with the main current. Either way, the strength of the eddy is on a continuum ranging from mild recirculation to a downright whirlpool.

In most "normal" eddies (those with none or only minimal upstream flow), aim to hit the eddy high, where the eddy recirculation is most crisp. Entering an eddy high helps ensure that you don't drift backward out the downstream end. To enter an eddy with strong upstream current, however, hit it low. The upstream

If you get caught at the eye of the eddy, think low! Keep a "flat boat" and be ready to low brace on either side.

eddy current can often be deceptively strong; enter too high and it may whip you up against the downstream side of the rock and cause a "pseudo-pin." Once you're sideways against the rock and in this turbulent area of the eddy, it's difficult to maneuver or gain enough speed to peel-out effectively. Aiming low also allows time to adjust your boat angle. The water is flowing fast enough that a few forward strokes will cause you to really fly upstream in no time, giving you plenty of speed for a peel-out or ferry.

When the recirculating current is particularly strong, it forms a whirlpool, where the middle is depressed and very turbulent and the outside is elevated and much tamer, though still fast-moving. To avoid this aquatic, dizzying, no man's land, hit the eddy/whirlpool low and travel upstream on the elevated, peripheral "ring" of smoother water. As with most eddy turns, lean to your inside throughout. If you find yourself aiming directly at the center of the whirlpool, paddle hard and lean upstream to break through the central turbulence and over to the "other side." The swirlies will have a tougher time grabbing your boat if you give them less chance to catch hold.

If you do find yourself stuck and spinning, stay calm and keep your boat flat. In a whirlpool, leaning won't help, as both ends and opposite edges of the boat are being grabbed simultaneously. Balance with your hips, and low brace if necessary. Wait until you're relatively stable and then paddle like mad when your boat is angled upstream and toward shore. The reason for waiting to spin into this boat position is twofold: First, it's difficult to exit almost any eddy, let alone a whirlpool, while pointing downstream; second, by starting an exit sprint when the boat is angled toward shore, you're *anticipating*—in a split-second the spinning eddy will carry you to an ideal exit spot. With good timing, you'll be at the right place to leave the eddy just as you've gotten the boat up to speed. If you misjudge and don't start paddling soon enough, don't worry. Go for another ride on the merry-go-round and get it right next time.

The Zig-Zag Approach

Stephen U'Ren

Probably the best way to run whitewater in control is to eddy-hop down the rapids. Zig-zagging from eddy to eddy allows you to break a complex stretch of whitewater into manageable morsels, and it gives you a chance to both scout ahead and regather the psyche and body. It's a lot of fun, and besides, if you want to get really good, you should practice catching eddies.

One of the simplest yet most valuable pieces of advice for running drops and getting into eddies is this: to get a chosen spot, begin from the other side. If you want to move river left and you start from the left side of the river, you'll have a harder time. It's easier to get river left when you begin from river right. This gives you an optional approach angle to catch a downstream eddy, and lets you tap into the river's energy, making things easier for you.

How? When you exit an eddy, the boat accelerates—downstream, of course, but you also get a definite cross-current boost. Why? Most rapids and all jets form where a river narrows, constricting the flow and forming compression waves (also known as tongues or "Vs" because of their diagonal, angular appearance). These waves often converge downstream at the V's point. Add power to your peel-out by catching the forceful flow running on the

sides of the V, and you can really zip across the current and into an eddy or down your chosen route. The key is to not let your boat turn too far downstream. Have plenty of smooth momentum as you exit the eddy. This strategy is invaluable when you have a critical line to stay on.

Let's say you're starting on the left and are forced to go down the left, or—even harder—you have to get even farther left of where you started. The diagonal compression waves that were so handy for crossing the stream now are a hindrance. If you have much cross-current speed or upstream angle you will get ferried too far into the main current to get back in time. On the other hand, you need to get enough beyond the eddy to escape the eddy line swirlies that can foul you up.

Exit fairly perpendicular to the eddy line so you'll turn downstream quickly. At the same time, make sure to have enough momentum to cross the eddy line in control. (The more turbulent the eddy line, the more speed you'll need.) Immediately place a bow draw (or Duffek) far out to your side and *pull* (don't cheat yourself of pulling distance—as many do—by placing your blade close to the boat). If you need to continue turning the bow downstream you can place the blade somewhat forward. But the main idea here is to pull, or

draw, the whole boat sideways. Avoid doing a sweep here; sweeps tend to accelerate you downstream rather than pull you laterally, and they can turn you too

much. After drawing, you can quickly change to a forward power stroke without taking the blade out of the water and wasting valuable time.

The Low Brace Turn: Stability on the Eddy Line

Claudia Kerckhoff-van Wijk

Although kayaks are a lot more stable than they might first appear, the paddlers who stay dry are the ones who know the proper technique to use in situations where overturning is a distinct possibility. Crossing an eddy line is one of these situations.

Whether you are a novice paddler or a seasoned expert, the low brace turn is a combination of moves that guarantees stability in your boat in all kinds of water. The low brace turn is the simplest and most stable maneuver for leaving the current and entering an eddy (eddy-in) or exiting into the current (eddy-out).

In teaching beginners and novice kayakers at our school, we have found that the low brace turn gives students valuable confidence in dealing with river currents. Not only does it help turn the boat, but it forces the paddler to lean the proper way when crossing the daunting eddy line.

But the low brace turn is not just for beginners. I often use it in big volume water. Reaching out over my low brace keeps my center of gravity low, sets a good boat edge, and gives me extra assurance in boiling, powerful water.

The following explanation uses the eddy-in situation to illustrate the successful low brace turn, which is a three-stroke combination of a forward sweep, a low brace, and a forward stroke.

As in all eddy turns, set a proper 45-degree boat angle aiming for the top of the eddy, where the eddy line is sharpest. Be sure to have good speed; low brace turns are only effective with speed.

To start the boat turning, place a forward sweep on the downstream side of the boat. In a forward sweep, the leading arm should be extended to the bow and the blade fully immersed in the water. Using the power face of the blade, push water away from the bow and around toward the stern in a wide, semicircular-circular motion. The wider you sweep, the better the boat will turn. In a low brace turn, the sweep should be started just before the bow of your kayak hits the eddy line. Switch to the main upstream side and place the low brace in the eddy. Make sure that your elbows are above the paddle shaft with your leading arm extended and your other arm bent over the cockpit. Lean both boat and body onto your paddle and hold the low brace for a count of two. Remember to look at your blade and to trust it; do not shy away from leaning on your paddle blade.

To help complete the turn, push your blade toward the bow as you might at the

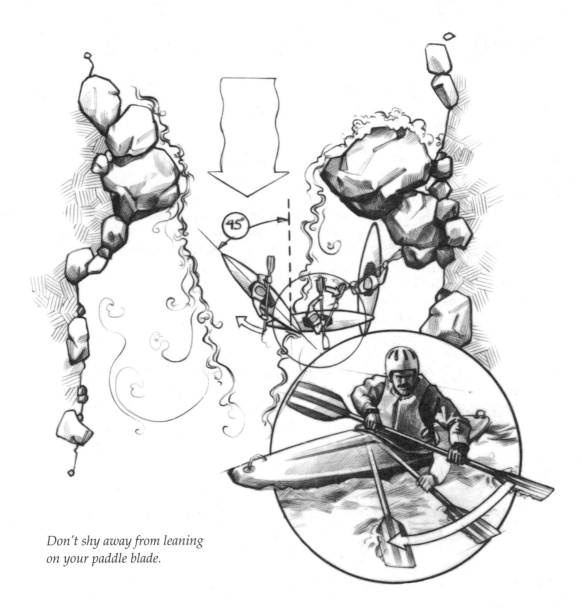

Don't shy away from leaning on your paddle blade.

end of a reverse sweep, causing the non-power face of the blade to travel in a semi-circular motion toward the bow. Then without removing your blade from the water, finish the low brace turn with a forward stroke. This ensures your spot in the eddy and keeps your boat from drifting downstream.

At this point you should be sitting pretty in the eddy, well positioned to take a small break from the current and to plan the next segment of your descent.

Getting from Hole to Eddy

Stephen U'Ren

Getting into an eddy that is "guarded" by an adjacent hole can be tricky, but it's easily manageable if you keep a few things in mind. Let's examine a couple of scenarios.

First, let's analyze a fairly common situation. An eddy you want to enter is bordered by a diagonal hole, such as Figure 1 on our illustrated river. You can usually find such an eddy behind a big rock at the bottom of a fairly steep, but not vertical, drop. This type of guardian hole is really just one side of a big, crashing "V" wave.

Because of its angle to the current, this type of hole can exaggerate any mistakes. If your angle has you pointed too far downstream, you'll glance off the diagonal hole downstream. Too much upstream angle and you'll abruptly spin out of control.

So to get deep in the eddy (and arrive in control), aim to punch the hole at an angle perpendicular to itself, regardless of how the main current is flowing. You will need plenty of momentum, so to get the proper angle and speed, start from the opposite shore, or if you're starting from the same side as the eddy, go quite wide across the main current and double back. Just before you punch the hole, lean the boat upstream, in anticipation of your eddy turn. (Realize that this is a very different situation from leaning upstream when leaving an eddy or dropping sideways into a hole.) Execute a powerful forward stroke on the upstream side just as you lean the boat, immediately before punching the hole. This stroke gives you last-second launching power, it prevents a spin-out, and it helps place the boat deep in the eddy. The result will literally launch you into the eddy.

Now, another scenario (see the illustration's second hole). You are paddling over a fairly steep drop with a hole at the bottom and you need to get immediately into a lateral eddy. You have to catch the eddy without letting the hole foul up your line. Turn too soon or too much to punch the eddy, and you'll drop sideways into the hole. If it's a small hole, a problem is unlikely. But if it's big, you may get stuck (much to your partners' amusement). If you punch the hole head-on and then turn and try to paddle for the eddy, chances are you'll miss the eddy, especially if the hole causes you to wobble or brace—however momentarily.

Thus, compromise: punch the hole diagonally. A 45-degree angle is a good rule of thumb, but it can vary. As much as possible, run the drop by starting from the opposite side to give yourself lots of lateral momentum. (You don't need to worry about downstream speed—you'll have plenty.) Hit the hole as close to the eddy as possible. Keep the boat flat or

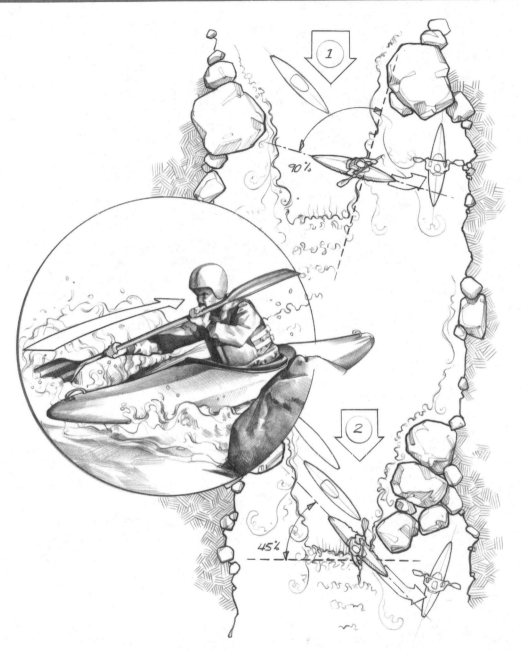

leaned downstream as you punch the hole—how much you lean depends on the size of the hole. Place a big, strong sweep in the hole's froth (inset) and you'll rocket into the eddy. Right after passing through the grabbiest part of the backwash, lean upstream as the eddy begins turning your bow.

Hole Surfing: Low Hands in the Hole!

Gordon Grant

Many people claim to like hole surfing, but most are secretly intimidated by those forces of nature and gravity that pummel them so. It doesn't have to be that way. Holes can be genuine fun if you follow these essentials:

KEEP A LIGHT PADDLE

Staying balanced in the hole depends upon maintaining an upright position over your boat with your upstream knee lifted. If you go into a hole with weight on your paddle, you'll stay stuck on a high brace and be unable to move to the corners of the hole. Once you have weight on the paddle, it is very hard to get it off. The only sure remedy is prevention: Go into the hole with good body position and your boat cocked up with the knee.

KEEP YOUR HANDS LOW

Good body positioning includes keeping your hands at shoulder level and below. Your arms should stay bent in relaxed Vs with the wrists rotated back to keep the blades of the paddle flat on the water. You can tell when people are getting desperate to get out of a hole, as their hands climb to head level and above. This puts more weight on the paddle, renders you immobile, and increases the likelihood of shoulder injury.

KEEP WORKING THE SWEEPS

The forward and back sweeps are your tickets to hole control. If you have the proper posture and knee lift, and you have kept a low, light paddle, you will be free to use sweeps to work the boat to the corner of the hole either to escape or to do 360s. Low hands make for stronger sweeps, both forward and back, because you are able to use your stomach and back muscles, as well as to apply power to your foot pegs for a really strong stroke.

KEEP USING MIGHTY MO

Momentum is your friend in working the corners. Many people get to the corner of a hole, are almost out, and then exhaust themselves by hanging there on a high brace. If you do feel yourself getting stuck on a corner, quickly use sweeps to go back across the hole. Your momentum will usually take you out the other side, especially if you've developed the balance to rely on your paddle for sweeps rather than braces.

These are the basics that apply to your local friendly play hole and to the Big One That Wants You For Real. Stick to these techniques and they'll see you out and smiling and encouraging others to go in. "Go on, it's great!"

Keep your hands low and your paddle light when hole surfing.

When your paddle climbs to face level, the hole has you immobile and you're risking shoulder injury.

39

Surfing the Tough Waves: It's a Vision Thing

Gordon Grant

The wave beckoned to be surfed: it was wide, it was fast, and an eddy fed back to it for repeat rides. But it was also unpredictable, with a "sweet spot" that kept shifting position and an erratic, steep break on the right. I had to work far too hard to stay on the wave, and my rides were short, frantic, and tiring. Sound familiar?

Then Phil Watford, a fellow kayak instructor who was watching my flailings, suggested that, next time on the wave, I fix my eyes on a beach that was just upstream.

I tried it, and the results were astounding: my boat stabilized, my stroke rate dropped by half, and I had the time I needed to carve easily back and forth. After a minute or so on the wave, I looked over at Phil, pointed toward the upstream beach and shouted, "What is up there?"

To my eyes, it was an empty gravel bar, but to my mind, I realized, it was a place to focus. I discovered that surfing more surgy, capricious waves may not be so much a matter of dexterity with the paddle as it is a matter of concentration.

Pick up your head, focus on an object upstream, and let your body naturally adjust to the wave.

If you're like most paddlers, when you're surfing a river wave you fix your gaze at the chaotic and disorienting sight of moving water and spray just upstream of your bow. This frenzy of rushing and shifting water, combined with the feeling of your boat buffeting in the current and the loud, constant sound of waves spilling over their crests, puts your mind on sensory overload, and your reactions are correspondingly rushed.

Better to focus on something fixed—a stationary landmark upstream—and let your body naturally adjust to the wave with the movements of knee and paddle that it already knows. Those adjustments will tend to bring you back in line with the object you're watching. It's like driving a car. You focus on objects ahead in the distance instead of looking just past the hood ornament at the pavement speeding toward you. You anticipate and naturally react when you need to turn, stop, adjust your speed, and so on. A similar thing will happen to you on the river. On a river, while many paddlers take a long view when paddling down a rapid, few—even the better ones—ever apply this concept to wave surfing. They should.

Should you ever look down your bow at the wave you are riding? Sure! When you enter the trough, you need to watch the angle of your boat as it crosses the edge of the wave. But once you're on the wave, lift your eyes and lock them onto an obvious target upstream. Sit upright and relaxed, and adjust the boat angle as you *feel* it change.

With a stationary focal point and basic surfing skills, you can set your sights on mastering more difficult waves. See for yourself!

River Boils

Stephen U'Ren

Most river boils are created when water rebounds off another object, be it a rock or water. Typically, water will pour over a drop, hit the bottom, and rebound up to the surface. Usually this process is somewhat irregular, leading to the characteristic "surginess" of boils. Turbulent eddies are rife with boils, where water pounds off itself, the bottom, and the bank in random fashion. You'll find boils upstream of rocks in current, where they're called pillows. Boils also form where two currents merge, and the greater the velocities, the more chaotic the results.

Usually boils are seen as an inconvenience, like some sort of river gremlin, existing only to push you off your path or force you into a sudden, wrenching brace.

Driving into an eddy with "boiling" current, bank off the boil's edge with an inside lean instead of charging into the boil.

But there are some strategies to avoid getting pushed around by these aquatic bullies, and in fact use them to your advantage.

Watch the boil to see if it's growing in size or shrinking. If the boil is growing, accelerate with a stroke or two and lean your boat so you present the boil with your hull, just like leaning into an eddy turn. This keeps the water on the boil's periphery (which is falling down under the surface) from grabbing your boat's edge. Finally, know where you want to go. Sounds simple, but if you have a planned direction you can at least attempt to keep your boat on a line and your speed up. Once you stall, a boil will grab you.

Let's examine some scenarios. Say you find a boil in the midst of an eddy. How do you do a crisp eddy turn without stalling out or spinning in some bizarre direction? Simply put, avoid the boil. Stay in the eddy proper and bank your boat off the boil's edge with an inside lean—the classic, eddy-turn lean. The boil's current will actually accelerate you through the turn.

Let's say you get too deep in the eddy and land on top of a violent, pulsating boil. Don't wrestle with it; steadily move yourself forward and sideways with a Duffek or a forward stroke with some side-draw component to it. Drawing your boat sideways through boiling current is difficult, but it may be your only option to avoid getting sucked into the thrashiest water high in the eddy. If you do get stuck, the boil will tend to push you laterally and then deposit you, without any speed, into a probably gnarly eddy line. You'll quickly be riding a buckin' bronco, if the eddy has any size.

Practice boil maneuvers. Start off on small ones to get the hang of it, and you'll be ready for the bigger ones.

Running Waterfalls

Stephen U'Ren

At some point, as your paddling experience grows, you'll be running waterfalls in the 6- to 10-foot range. There are many types of waterfalls, but the basic strategies for running them successfully are universal.

The most universal strategy is scouting. Only rarely will you want to run a drop sight-unseen, even on a river that's familiar to you. (After all, a river's hydraulics can change dramatically over a brief period of time.) One bank—or the portage route—may not offer the best vantage point. You may need to ferry to the other bank to assess the situation more effectively. Take the time and effort to scout whenever you or someone in your party has even a bit of doubt. It will go a long way toward keeping your confidence—and body—intact.

When you scout a waterfall, judge the difficulty of a drop not only by how high it is but by how safely you can deal with what's below the falls—the bottom pool and the recirculating hydraulic.

In general, the more shallow the bottom pool, the less severe the hole, and vice versa. The condition of the bottom pool and stopper hole can be difficult to gauge, even for those experienced at reading holes and water aeration patterns. Ideally, you'd like the pool to be at least deeper than the length of your boat. But in reality, you can only look for the obvious, like the volume of water pouring over the falls in relation to the height of the falls, the size and shape of the hole at the bottom, and rocks or outcroppings that could cause a bow-pin or piton.

Let's say you're faced with a 10-foot, nearly vertical drop with a good chute of fast water running at almost midstream. At the landing, a medium-sized hole is frothing, surging, boiling—definitely something to avoid. A "ski jump" can carry you beyond the worst of the hole. The goal of ski jumping is to land the boat fairly flat in the pool at the bottom with some downstream speed. Landing flat and without speed in slack water is a good way to compress your vertebrae.

Visualizing your run from shore will minimize the chances of last-minute corrections on the water. As you consider whether to run or walk the falls, ask yourself these questions: Is there enough room to make a running start? Are there any obstacles (including funny water) that might hinder your line or speed? Will you be able to recognize them from upstream, in your boat? What line over the falls will you take to avoid obstacles at the bottom? At the lip, will anything interfere with your launch?

Let's say you decide to run the falls. As you approach the edge, time your final forward stroke so you place the blade right at the lip of the drop. As you power through your last stroke, thrust out with

As you power through your last stroke, thrust out with your hips and vault yourself over the edge. Flex your abdominals and lift with your knees to keep your bow up; lean slightly forward and follow through with your forward paddling rhythm.

your hips and vault yourself over the edge. While airborne, flex your abdominal muscles and lift with your knees to keep your bow up (this is to avoid deep immersion on landing). Lean slightly forward and follow through with your forward paddling rhythm. This helps maintain your forward momentum, keeps your paddle shaft away from your face, and sets your blade for the next stroke when you land. That next "stroke" will act as a natural low brace.

If the hole is too big or the pool too shallow for straight-ahead ski jumping, the simplest line is to run the drop diago-nally from one side (the one above the drop) to the other (the one below the drop). At speed, you still will avoid most of the hole, and you can punch surprisingly big holes because the vertical drop gives the boat so much momentum. (Back-enders are also less common with the diagonal approach.) Aim correctly and you'll land on the shoulder of the hole, in slower water, or in an eddy. You do not, however, want to go over the falls sideways without any cross-current momentum. Without speed, the boat will plunge and list over while airborne, setting you up for a serious thrashing.

A Balanced Approach

Gordon Grant

Don't the experts make it look easy? Carving out of eddy turns, or doing hands-only 360s in holes, they look relaxed in their boats, serene amidst the turbulence of whitewater. So why does it take so long to find that balance for ourselves?

Because we interfere with simplicity. We spend our time trying to develop some new "advanced" stroke and miss the obvious: expertise comes from executing the basics in all situations, and the most basic of basics is to stay balanced in your boat.

How? Here's a simple, inelegant answer: keep your head over your butt. Ah, but this message contains an elegant truth; if your head stays over your center and in the center of the boat, you stay in balance. Here are some exercises with which, beginner or advanced, you can improve your balance and free yourself from a mistaken reliance on the paddle for support.

On flatwater—relax. Sit upright in your kayak. Wiggle the boat from side to side by lifting alternate knees. As long as you keep your head centered, note how much you can rock the boat up on edge without losing a sense of stability. Practice the feel of lifting the boat up as high as possible, just to the balance point, first with the right knee and then the left. If you feel yourself losing balance, simply lift with the knee you are falling toward and flop the boat down flat. This little drill sets up the proper response to instability; you regain balance by pulling the boat under you with your knees, rather than by slapping on the water with your paddle.

To prove my point about balance, try sitting upright again. This time move your head about eight inches to the left or right, over the edge of the boat. Can you feel gravity pulling you over further? Feel the instability, the water licking its lips in anticipation of your imminent head-first arrival. I rest my case.

On whitewater—find a spot where a jet of current runs into a pool, a safe spot where you can experiment. Paddle out of the eddy at the angle you normally would take, but use your paddle only for power—not bracing. As your feet cross the eddy line, rotate your torso in the direction you are turning. If you twist to the right, you naturally tend to pull up slightly with your left knee. Be aware of this pressure and increase or relax it depending on how much lift you need. Once your boat is fully out in the current and going the same speed as the water, you can relax the pressure on the knee and set the boat down flat. Do this drill repeatedly, peeling out on both sides of the river to gain complete comfort with left and right knee lifts. Do you need to lean hard downstream? No. Rotate rather than lean. That will keep the boat under you.

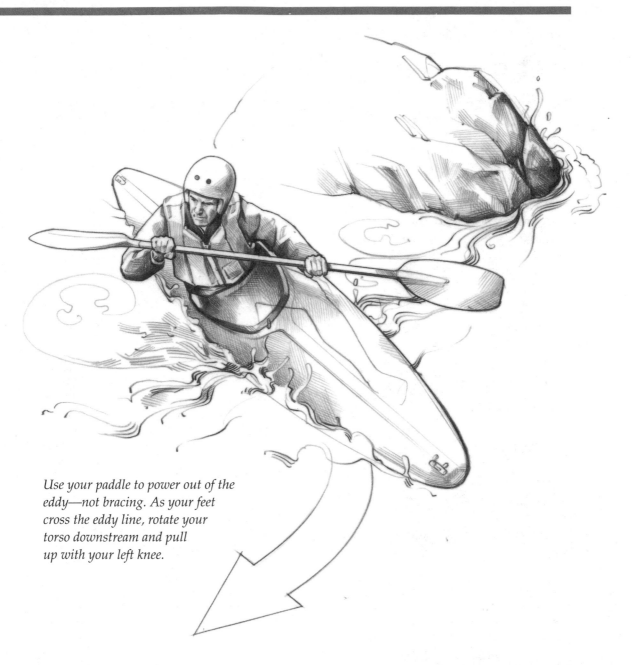

Use your paddle to power out of the eddy—not bracing. As your feet cross the eddy line, rotate your torso downstream and pull up with your left knee.

All this seem too easy for you? Do it backwards! Still a breeze? Great! Get rid of the paddle. Repeated drills such as this will give you the balanced seat of the expert kayakers and set you up to learn all those dazzling hole riding maneuvers about which you've been fantasizing. Get going. Throw that crutch away!

Let the Games Begin! Kayaking Games for Fun Learning

Claudia Kerckhoff-van Wijk

Playing in your boat is an ideal way to improve balance and paddle coordination (without tedious practice). At the Madawaska Kanu Centre, we like to introduce our students to a variety of games they can play. Apart from just having fun, there are a number of reasons for this: it is a low pressure way to introduce kids to the sport of paddling; it is a nonthreatening way to help nervous people feel comfortable in the water; by concentrating on the game, new paddlers increase their confidence of getting in and out of their boats.

THE KAYAK STAR

This game is a lot easier to perform with 12 or more kayakers. The aim is to have all the paddlers standing up in their boats at the same time.

How to Play. All paddlers pull their bows together in a circle. Each paddler then removes his or her sprayskirt and sits on the back of the boat, wedging his or her feet firmly in the seat. Each paddler then must reach out and put his or her arms around the shoulders of the paddlers to his or her left and right. So far so good. The tricky part comes once everyone is in this position, and someone calls out the countdown; on three, everyone tries to stand up in his or her boat!

The idea is to use each other's shoulders for balance and support as you stand. It can be a wobbly exercise and usually a wet one as well, but it is good fun for everyone.

KAYAK POLO

This game is a serious sport in Britain, where it is played competitively in indoor swimming pools at colleges and canoe clubs. Our version is a little less competitive and a lot tamer. We also opt for the no-paddle version to reduce the risk of injuries. The general aim is similar to water polo, where teams pass the ball and shoot it into their opponent's goal.

This game is best played on flatwater, either in a swimming pool, on a lake, or in the large pools between rapids. All you need is a net, which can take many forms: either float two plastic bottles anchored with a rope and a rock to make the two goal posts, or keep the concept simple and choose two significant points on the shore (like a stump or hanging tree) at each end of the playing area. The ball shot past this point scores a goal.

Rules. The rules are simple and geared to safety. Boat holding is not allowed. Players have to travel with the ball touching the water (they are not allowed to place it on the sprayskirt), which encourages passing and ensures that everyone will get to play. The most important rule of the game is to help others roll up if they overturn.

How to Play. Divide your group into two teams, and then have someone throw the ball into the center of the playing area. This is the face-off that will start the game. The object of the game is to pass the ball from teammate to teammate, trying to advance to the other team's net.

If the other team has control of the ball, the object is to steal it back by intercepting the ball in a mid-air pass or by aggressively grabbing it out of their hands.

This is where a paddler could tip over. If this happens and the person does not have a hand-roll, then immediately position your boat for a bow rescue. Remember, your team gets the ball if you help someone up.

When you get close enough to the other team's goal, shoot the ball in. Each goal is worth a point, and the first team to get five points wins the game.

Think of these games the next time you are with a gang of paddlers on a stretch of flatwater. Games are a great way to break the ice with a new group or can be used as a warm-up exercise before an intense day of paddling.

Kayak polo is one of many games to build skill and confidence.

Return of the English Gate

Gordon Grant

The old saying is that it is not practice that makes perfect, rather, "perfect practice makes perfect." The English gate is a means of developing mastery of every stroke used by whitewater kayakers, and presence of mind, as well. The gate can be hung anywhere, and is often used in winter pool training. Nine passes are made through the gate: five forward and four reverse, as well as four rolls. Though designed and used by racers, this exercise still has direct usefulness for recreational boaters in developing dexterity, fitness, and deeply ingrained good habits that will enhance your enjoyment of the river.

Your emphasis in English gate drills should be on smoothness and precision, rather than speed. You can choose your stroke: forward strokes, sweeps, bow draws or Duffek, reverse and reverse sweeps, but your main purpose is to maintain a continuous movement with the fewest strokes possible. Ideally, one should learn the gate, and do it dozens of times at a slow rhythm, in order to imprint techni-cally correct strokes in your consciousness. If you perform your strokes in a rushed and sloppy manner, those are the strokes you will perform under pressure. Go slowly. Have a friend critique you or, best of all, video your workout so that you can watch and specifically analyze the effectiveness of your stroke.

The diagram here sets forth the patterns you must learn. To avoid confusion, remember the following: Phases III and IV require going backward through the gate. You will finish the sequence in the identical position to starting it—facing the gate. Learn each phase completely before you move onto the next phase. Do not be concerned if it takes you a long time to do this. What you are seeking is long-term improvement. If you rush in attempting to complete this sequence, you will short-circuit the whole process. Think of it as Tai Chi for whitewater. Relax, focus on the movements, and visualize applying them on your favorite stretch of river.

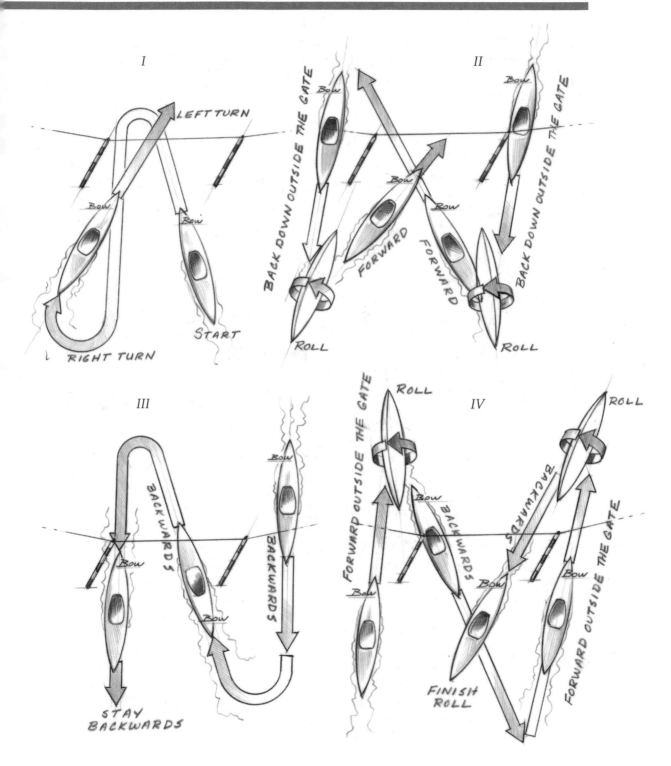

I

LEFT TURN

Bow

Bow

START

RIGHT TURN

II

BACK DOWN OUTSIDE THE GATE

BACK DOWN OUTSIDE THE GATE

Bow

Bow

Bow

Bow

FORWARD

FORWARD

ROLL

ROLL

III

BACKWARDS

BACKWARDS

Bow

Bow

Bow

STAY BACKWARDS

IV

ROLL

ROLL

FORWARD OUTSIDE THE GATE

FORWARD OUTSIDE THE GATE

BACKWARDS

BACKWARDS

Bow

Bow

Bow

Bow

FINISH ROLL

51

The Slalom Upstream Gate

Stephen U'Ren

A regulation 25-gate slalom course contains a minimum of six upstream gates (so-called "ups"), putting the emphasis on a move which is equally critical to your success in making any controlled white-water descent. The goal is to power into an eddy and move upstream through a slalom gate using only two strokes: a Duffek to turn the boat in the eddy, and a second stroke, usually a sweep, to exit the eddy. Doing this combines power, precision, and efficiency all in one move.

A flatwater site may be the best place to begin, but for the sake of example, let's go right to the river. Start by hanging one gate (two 3-foot-long poles suspended 3 feet apart, their ends about 6 inches off the water) over the middle of a medium-sized eddy with crisp, well-defined eddy lines.

The key to running an upstream gate is your approach. Take a wide, arcing approach to the eddy and aim to hit the eddy line at a 90-degree angle. This slightly longer, wider, but smoother approach is faster than coming straight down on top of the eddy and turning into it at the last second because it allows you to keep up your boat speed.

If the approach to the eddy is too tight to make a wide turn, set your angle with a C-stroke, so called because C-1 slalom racers use it (not to be confused with the C-stroke solo open canoe paddlers use). The C-stroke, used while you're still in the main current, will turn your bow toward the eddy line without decreasing your momentum the way a sweep does. Think of the C-stroke as a sort of Duffek that you draw toward your feet. Place the blade far out to your upstream side at about 45 degrees to the boat's long axis and draw it toward your bow. Keep the blade slightly closed (a "closed" blade is one where the power face faces you), almost parallel to the boat. You won't feel much resistance if you're doing it right.

Either way, reach far forward and use a power stroke on your downstream side to pierce the eddy line at a right angle. If your approach angle is correct, the eddy current and the force of the stroke will turn the boat plenty when it's in the eddy. A full-fledged sweep may turn the boat too much, causing it to stall.

Your target area in the eddy is the "pocket" deep in the eddy and just below the gate, so that you won't have to come up through the gate any more than necessary. Reach way out and insert the Duffek when you're in line with the middle of the gate. When you pull on the blade and pivot the boat around it, your body should have traveled almost to the outside pole and your boat should already be angled toward the gate. As with the C-stroke, keep the blade angle closed. A closed blade allows the fastest, most efficient turn. If you're in the right spot, the

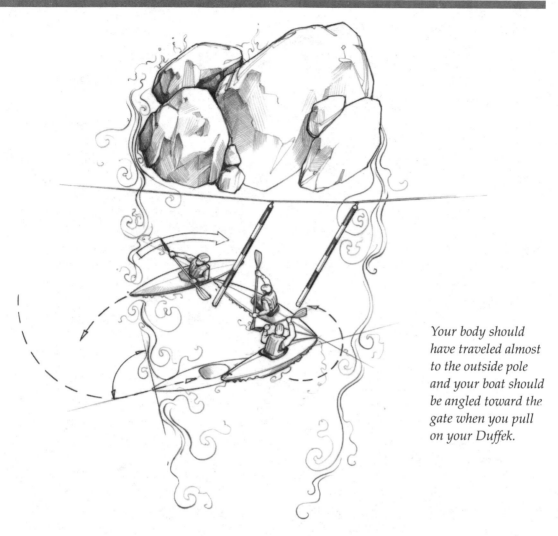

Your body should have traveled almost to the outside pole and your boat should be angled toward the gate when you pull on your Duffek.

eddy line will do most of the work to turn the boat. Only in a slack eddy will you need to open up the blade for additional turning power.

Just before your boat speed dwindles from the tail end of your Duffek, convert your Duffek to a forward stroke and pull your boat between the poles. As your body passes through the gate, place your exit stroke—a sweep—on your other side. If you need to ferry and not peel out, don't come as close to the inside pole; instead,

maintain your angle as you pass through the gate and start your ferry.

As the illustration shows, the idea is to cut a path so you come close to the outside pole with your right shoulder as you come up through the gate, and close to the inside pole with the left shoulder as you exit.

Practice entering and exiting using only two strokes, and experiment to develop efficiency and precision in your technique.

And of course, try not to touch the poles.

Maximize Your Pool Time

Claudia Kerckhoff-van Wijk

It's the dead of winter, cold and snowing, but that doesn't mean that you have to give up paddling. An indoor swimming pool lets you practice your paddling strokes in the off season. Warm and clear, it's the ideal setting for "winter games" and to practice your braces and the Eskimo roll.

Only about 10 paddlers can be accommodated in a 25-meter pool, so organization of your pool session is essential. Set up the shallow end of the pool for rolling practice, which leaves the deep end for stroke work. This allows two groups to work each area simultaneously. A group leader should set an agenda in advance, splitting up the group and keeping an eye on the time allotted for the session.

For stroke work, create a "pretend" eddy in the deep end of the pool. A slalom gate hanging in the deep end can be visualized as a rock where an eddy is formed. Paddlers can use this gate to practice their peel-outs and eddy turns. Form a line and practice follow-the-leader through the gate or work on the English gate. Or, one of my favorites, practice sculling around one pole without removing the paddle from the water. An excellent forward stroke exercise is to tie two sterns together and have a tug-of-war, where each paddler tries to pull the other through the gate. Many types of competitions and exercises can evolve around just one gate. Keep track of each paddler's times and compare them monthly to see if there is an improvement.

If one of your leaders is a strong technician or an experienced instructor, get feedback on posture and strokes during these sessions. If possible, use a video camera with slow-motion playback to analyze a paddler's execution. Pool sessions are the time to work on proper technique and eliminate sloppy habits; it's a great environment for concentrating on individual skills.

For more fun in the deep end, try seal launching off the side of the pool, or try pirouettes and enders. Have a fellow paddler stand on the side of the pool and lift your stern into the air over your head in a straight or twisting motion to perform a pirouette. (Be sure to secure the pool management's approval beforehand!)

Rolling—There are ways to ease beginners through the "fear-and-loathing" phase of the Eskimo roll. With kids, especially, try using games and horseplay aimed at getting beginners wet and familiar with the kayak. Fill boats with water, and coax kayakers to climb into already semi-submerged boats. Where's the fear of tipping over when you're already in the water?

Here are a few more ideas for distracting beginner paddlers to get them comfortable in the water, while having fun. Try having them pick up an object off the bottom of the pool and then rolling up. Or climb into the boat while it is upside down

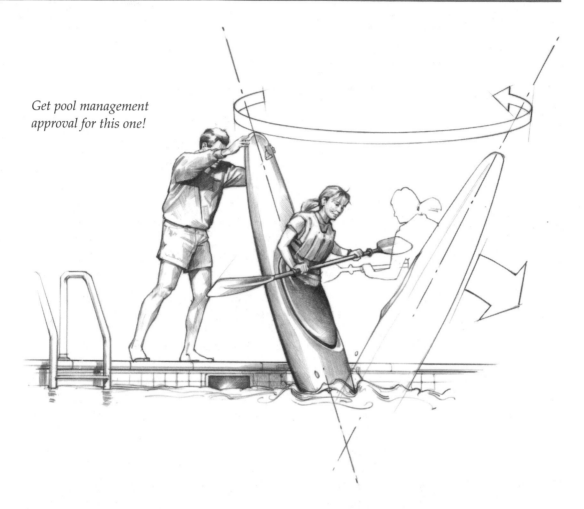

Get pool management approval for this one!

and then roll up. Have them fall upside down in the deep end; then, put their head into the cockpit to breathe, climb into their boat, and roll it back up, without ever surfacing. Another "presence of mind" drill is to have them fall over and pass the paddle over the hull of the kayak to roll up on the opposite side. Learning to react to a surprise tipover is good practice. Try the "washing machine." Have someone stand in the pool at the kayak stern and tip the boat over without warning of when, or which way, the boat is going over. In a

pool, you can always swim to your paddle or to the edge of the pool and roll up. In fact, the edge of the pool is a great place to work on your hip snap, an essential part of a good roll.

Swimming pools are not made for kayaking, so their use is a privilege. Show respect by thoroughly cleaning your boat of leaves and sand before the session. By cooperating with pool management, even offering introductory clinics to pool staff, you will enjoy this off-season playground for many seasons to come.

Patterns of Grace for Moments of Stress

Gordon Grant

Be forewarned: this article reveals no technique or specific strokes. Instead, it focuses on an improvement approach taken by too few recreational paddlers.

There are very few kayak strokes to learn; what separates the brilliant experts from the rest of us mortals is that the experts simply execute those strokes in all situations, no matter how intense or perilous. Why can't the rest of us do that?

The answer is simple: fear short-circuits our ability to perform. Under stress, we naturally revert to basic patterns of movement. If those technically correct strokes are not ingrained in us, then our strokes under stress mirror that basic imperfection. Watch most paddlers at their personal limits, whether class III or V, and you will notice a deterioration of technique in all but the best. Again, why? The way most paddlers learn the sport is through a progression onto more difficult rivers. After a while paddling class II, a person decides to move up to class III, and so on. This may seem logical, but what happens is that people put themselves into more stressful situations without taking the necessary time to deeply imprint the technical skills needed to handle those situations well. Recent training studies in other "risk" sports like rock climbing have shown that the development of new physical movements and skills can only take place when the athlete is fresh, in a safe environment, and free from fear. This patterning of movement is called acquiring "engrams." For further reading on this, I refer you to the excellent book *Performance Rock Climbing* by Dale Goddard and Udo Neumann (Stackpole Books).

Kayak racers have long known this, and among other exercises, will do "marathons," where they run at slow speed through a sequence of gates for thirty minutes to an hour nonstop. They are deeply imprinting mental and muscular connections that will be there for them when moving at a top speed on a race course.

What do rock climbers and slalom racers have to do with recreational boating, you may ask? We just want to play, right? Take note: It is no fluke that the recent Ocoee Rodeo World Championships were won by two slalom racers, Eric Jackson and Scott Shipley, neither of whom had spent a fraction of the time practicing at Hell Hole that the other competitors had. What they took into the hole with them were patterns of movement with which they could adapt to any situation.

Perfect your techniques in a non-stressful environment. You'll have the moves when you need them.

Interested? Try the following on your next river trip. Spend at least half an hour early in the trip concentrating on smooth, precise execution of basic moves in one spot. Do eddy turns, peel-outs, and ferries (front and back), with specific attention paid to each stroke. If you only have flatwater near your home on which to practice, consider hanging five gates in an "X" pattern. You can spend time moving through this course at slow to moderate speed, and follow a pattern that will utilize every turning stroke in kayaking. If you are pressed for space, hang a single

gate and practice the English gate pattern through it. This is a pattern of movement through and around the gate that also involves every stroke commonly used in boating, including rolls. If you don't have the site to hang gates, try anchored milk jugs around which to maneuver.

If you practice in this manner for an hour a week over the next few months, I guarantee you will notice the difference in your paddling on your next whitewater outing. You'll be calmer, your boat will go where you want it to, and even in unfamiliar rapids, you'll feel you've come home.

Whitewater Glossary

Boil: Swirly or unpredictable currents pushing to the surface.

Bony: Run or rapid requiring lots of maneuvering because of the abundance of obstacles, mostly rocks.

Boof: Driving your boat for a mini-launch over a shallow ledge or rock.

Brace: Paddling technique using downward and sweeping strokes to stabilize a tipping canoe or kayak.

Broach: Occurs when a canoe or kayak becomes caught in the current against an obstruction and turned sideways. Can result in severe damage as the current's force wraps the boat around the obstruction.

CFS: Cubic Feet per Second. Measurement of velocity of water flow at a given point in a river. Will vary according to water level and gradient of riverbed.

Class I–VI: International standard classification system for rating the difficulty of fast-moving water.

Confluence: The junction of two rivers or forks of a river.

Control Hand: "Fixed" hand, left or right, depending on the offset of the blades on a kayak paddle.

Curler: A large wave, usually at the bottom of a drop, with a crest that spills upon its upstream slope. May be a surfing site.

Drop: A short, well-defined rapid or section of a rapid. Named for the abrupt drop in elevation between the top and bottom of the rapid.

Eddy: The area behind or downstream of an obstruction in the main current, where water swirls counter to that of the main flow.

Eddy In: To enter an eddy.

Eddy Line: The transitional area between main current and eddy current.

Eddy Out: To exit an eddy. *See* Peel Out.

Ender: A play maneuver enacted by nosing the bow into a vertical hydraulic that forces the bow down and deep and the stern up, which results in the boat popping vertically upward. Good fun.

Ferry: A maneuver used to cross a current with little or no downstream travel. Utilizes the current's force to move boat laterally.

Float Bag: The most common form of supplemental flotation in canoes and kayaks.

Gauge Height: For measuring water levels at one or more locations. Reference point used with CFS (or in lieu of).

Grab Loop: Grab-handle threaded through bow/stern stems of a kayak or canoe. Useful as carry-handles and for catching swimmers.

Gradient: The steepness of a riverbed over a specified distance, usually per mile. Along with CFS and water-level information, this helps paddlers draw a picture of a river's difficulty. *See* CFS and Class I–VI.

Hair: Dangerous and difficult whitewater.

Hair Boating: Paddling in dangerous and difficult whitewater.

Haystacks: Big standing waves in a wave "train" following a drop.

Headwall: A steep cliff where the main channel of the river drives against it at a 90-degree angle.

Hole: Benign to severe, a hole is created when the river current drops over a rock or ledge and circulates instead of continuing its downstream flow. A significant feature because it offers either play opportunities or danger, depending on the circulating power of the hole.

Horizon Line: Usually indicates a falls or steep drop. The route, if there is one, is not apparent. Time to exit and scout.

Hydraulic: A water formation following a sudden drop in the riverbed or drop over an obstruction that creates a powerful circulating force at the base. The circulating pressure of a powerful hydraulic can hold boats and paddlers for indeterminate lengths of time. *See* Hole.

Hypothermia: The cold water hazard for paddlers. Prolonged exposure can lead to incapacitation and eventually death as body core temperature drops below 80 degrees.

Maytag: Being stuck in a hole and thrashed about as if in a washing machine. Usually not fun.

Mystery Move: A mysterious and lengthy disappearance underwater, then reappearance to the surface in an entirely different location. Fun, especially when intentional.

Pearl: To bury the nose of a kayak in a wave.

Peel Out: The act of leaving an eddy and entering the main current; bow catches the main current and quickly swings the boat downstream.

PFD: Personal Flotation Device. The buoyancy vest required by law for every passenger on all water craft and your most important life-saving tool.

Pin: Being stuck between the current and the riverbed or an obstruction such as a rock or log and being unable to dislodge. Not fun; possibly deadly.

Pirouette: A boat-and-paddler spin effected while popping vertical in a kayak during an "ender." *See* Ender.

Piton: To collide nose-first with an obstacle above or below the water; forces the paddler to the nose of the boat.

Portage: To carry boats and gear around a difficult rapid or series of rapids.

Put-in: Starting place of a river trip, where you put your boat on the river to begin a run or a trip.

Ramp: Point in a rapid where water constricts/pools before dropping (spilling) downstream through a channel.

River Left: The left-hand side of a river when looking downriver.

River Right: The right-hand side of a river when looking downriver.

Roll: A move requiring a paddle stroke and body snap to right oneself from a tipover while staying in the boat. Common techniques are the sweep and Eskimo rolls.

Roostertail: A fountain of water that explodes off a submerged obstacle.

Shuttle: Travel between the put-in and take-out. One-vehicle outings require logistical foresight using options such as bicycling, walking, hitchhiking, etc., to return to vehicle at put-in.

Side Surf: A play move in a benign hole in which paddler uses countervailing forces of downstream current and upstream hydraulic.

Sprayskirt (or Spray Deck): A neoprene or nylon accessory that fits around the waist of the paddler and the cockpit lip of canoe or kayak for a watertight closure.

Squirt Boat: An extremely low-volume (small) kayak that uses the underwater river currents.

Standing Waves: Big waves that often indicate the main channel. *See* Haystacks.

Strainer: An obstruction in the water that allows the current to pass through but stops any object floating or submerged. Dangerous.

Surfing: Technique for riding large waves on a river. Good fun.

Take-out: Ending point of a paddling trip, where the boats are finally taken from the water.

Technical: A rapid that requires deft and skillful maneuvering because of frequent obstructions. Also, specific, difficult-to-master paddling techniques.

Throw Bag: Rescue device incorporating a long rope coiled inside a nylon bag, to be thrown while holding one rope end.

Tongue: A smooth V indicating the route through a drop. *See* Ramp.

Undercut: An overhanging rock or ledge with water flowing underneath it. A serious hazard.

Waterfall: A major drop in a riverbed, usually more than six feet high.

Wave Train: A series of standing waves. *See* Haystacks.

Canoe & Kayak Subscription Information

For more than 24 years, *Canoe & Kayak* magazine has been the world's leading paddlesports publication and resource for canoeing, kayaking and the full range of paddlesports. Full-color features capture both the beauty and tranquillity of the sport as well as the adventure and excitement—from family weekend trips to world expeditions, from calm water touring to whitewater adventures.

Published six times a year, *Canoe & Kayak* includes regular sections on technique, equipment reviews, services, destinations, health and fitness, and the environment, along with features about the people, ideas, issues, and events that shape the growing sport of paddling. Subscription includes the annual Buyer's Guide in the December issue.

To subscribe, call 1-800-678-5432, and ask for the "Subscription Special," (six issues for $15) or write: *Canoe & Kayak* magazine, P.O. Box 7011, Red Oak, IA 51591-4011.